STARTERS

Festivals

Lynn Huggins-Cooper

Bony bodies

Text copyright © Lynn Huggins-Cooper 2004

Language consultant: Andrew Burrell
Subject consultant: Lisa Kassapian
Design: Perry Tate Design
Picture research: Glass Onion Pictures

Published in Great Britain in 2004
by Hodder Wayland, an imprint of
Hodder Children's Books

This paperback edition published in 2007 by Wayland,
an imprint of Hachette Children's Books.

The publishers would like to thank the following for allowing us to reproduce their
pictures in this book: Wayland Picture Library; 4, 8, 20, 21 (top), 22 / Hutchison
Picture Library; 15 / James Davis Travel Photography; 21 (bottom) / Corbis; cover,
title page, 6, 7, 8, 9 (top), 12, 13, 14, 16, 18 (bottom) / Impact; 17, Getty Images; 18
(top) / AI Pix; 22 (top), 23 / Andes Press Agency; 9 / Zul Mukhida; 19 / Christine
Osborne Pictures; 5, 10 (bottom), 11, 14 (bottom)

A catalogue record for this book is available from the British Library.

ISBN-10: 0 7502 4548 4
ISBN-13: 978 0 7502 4548 7

Printed and bound in China

Wayland,
an imprint of Hachette Children's Books
338 Euston Road, London NW1 3BH

Contents

Party people!

People all over the world love to celebrate and have festivals.

Many people celebrate on their birthday, with cake, presents, balloons and parties.

Have you ever been to a birthday party?

At Christmas, many people also have parties and put up decorations. Christian people go to church to celebrate the story of the birth of Jesus.

Beautiful decorations are hung on a Christmas tree.

Happy New Year!

Chinese New Year is celebrated in February with firecrackers, lion dancers and dragons.

On Rosh Hashannah, in September or October, Jewish people celebrate new beginnings.

Sweet honey cakes are eaten as a wish for a sweet year!

Baisakhi is the name of the Sikh New Year. It is celebrated on 13th April. In Punjab, India, people dance to music and give sweets to their friends and family.

Harvest Time

Christian Harvest festivals celebrate the good things God gives to people. Churches are decorated with flowers, fruit and vegetables.

In Ghana and Nigeria, people celebrate the Yam Festival. They dress in traditional clothes and thank the Gods for their food.

During the Jewish festival of Succoth, people also give thanks to God for the harvest. They build special tents or huts in the garden, called 'succah'.

People decorate their succah with harvest foods.

Hanukkah is a festival that lasts eight days. Jewish people light an extra candle every night.

The candles sit in a holder called a 'Menorah'.

During the festival of Holi, Hindu people throw colourful powders and water about to make everything bright!

Everyone is covered in colour!

Diwali is the festival of lights celebrated by Hindu and Sikh people. People light up beautiful lamps and eat special food.

Sparklers and fireworks light up the sky.

May Day is on 1st May. It is celebrated in parts of England by people dancing with ribbons around a maypole. It celebrates springtime and the way plants start to grow.

The ribbons become tied around the pole by the dancers.

Apple Day
is a festival
in Autumn.
People in some
countries visit orchards to
taste different sorts of apple.

Thanksgiving celebrates the Autumn
harvest in the USA. Some families eat a
delicious meal and give thanks.

This special turkey
is decorated with
seasonal fruits
and herbs.

Spooky Festivals

In Britain and North America, Halloween is celebrated on 31st October.

Scary faces are carved into pumpkin lanterns.

Some people dress in spooky costumes. They go trick or treating to collect sweets from people they know.

In Mexico, Dias de los Muertos is celebrated on 31st October, when people remember relatives who have died.

They cook delicious meals, and eat sugar skeletons and coffins!

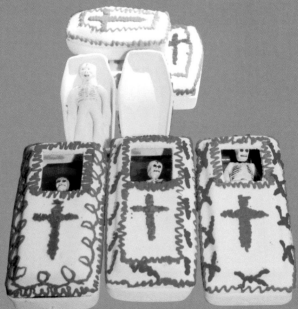

On 5th May, some Japanese families celebrate Tango-no-Sekku, the Boys' Festival.

For each son, a colourful paper fish is hung up outside the house.

The Japanese Girls' Festival on 3rd March, is called Hina Matsuri. Houses are decorated with dolls and rice dumplings are eaten.

Raksha Bandan is a Hindu festival when brothers and sisters show their love for each other.

This girl has made a rakhi bracelet for her brother to show how much she loves him.

Valentine's Day is on 14th February. People in many places give each other cards and presents to say 'I love you'.

Kwanzaa is an African American holiday. Houses are decorated with black, red and green streamers. People light candles and eat special food.

Eid-ul-Fitr is an important Muslim festival where families and friends give presents and money as gifts. Gifts of money are also given to poor people.

This girl is giving Eid presents to her sister.

Easter

Easter is celebrated by Christians all over the world. Mardi Gras is a bright, colourful festival held just before the Easter season begins.

People make Easter bonnets and dress up for parades.

In Britain, people eat pancakes on Shrove Tuesday. Some people have pancake races, tossing a pancake in the air!

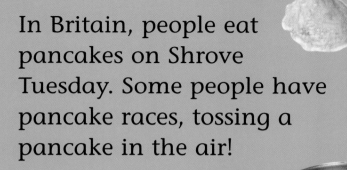

On Easter Sunday, Christians go to church and a special candle is lit.

Some people celebrate with Easter egg hunts and chocolate bunnies!

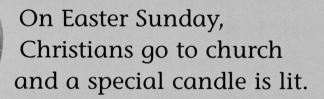

Festivals everywhere!

People all over the world enjoy festivals and celebrations! They enjoy dressing in special clothes and costumes.

They enjoy making and eating delicious festival food.

And they all enjoy parties and colourful celebrations!

Which festivals do your family celebrate?

Celebrate When people have parties and parades to mark special days. **4, 5**

Costume Special, decorated clothes people wear when they are in parades and at parties. **14, 22**

Decorations Streamers, special pictures and ornaments used to make places pretty for special days. **5, 8, 18**

Festival A time to celebrate with singing, dancing, special food and giving thanks for the good things we have. **4, 22, 23**

Harvest When farmers collect their crops and people celebrate and give thanks for the food they have. **8, 9, 13**

Orchard Where apple trees are grown. **13**

Parade A celebration when people dress in special clothes and move down the street, singing and dancing. **20**

Succah Special tents or huts built outside by Jewish people during Succoth. **9**